A LION

Praise for *A Lion*

Pleasure—pleasure for pleasure's sake, and pleasure in the face of trouble and sorrow, the limitless yes—that is what poetry was made for. Remember Sappho, kids? Remember Adelia Prado and Frank O'Hara? For certain folk, pleasure is the shape that courage takes in the body—they have heart, "that animal in an animal." The best of these folkies—and Sarah Stickney is surely one—have all the wit and slyness needed to keep that heart alive and pumping, no matter what. Always welcoming, sometimes ruefully ironic, these poems have plenty of trouble in mind, the basic human thing you might say, being too honest to avoid it, but they insist over and over on delight— in touch, in talk and laughter, in food and drink, in solitude, in vulnerability, even in misery. There is delight even in misery, did you know that? Read this book, and it will show you where. It'll give you the how and why. The book is so damn good.

—David Rivard

Poetry likes to be serious about casual matters like flowers and coffee, revealing them to mean more than they first appear, squeezing out the unconscious via the indirection of description. But Sarah Stickney's poetry performs poetry's other gambit— to be (apparently) casual about serious matters, reminding us of all the things we can't seem to be able to say even if they're as obvious as flowers and coffee.... Stickney's concise lyrics offer quick takes and sharp judgments as they make available interior conversations whose uncanny logic kicks back against civilization itself. What might be most anachronistic—and most vital—about this book is that Stickney writes as a woman interested in women, not only erotically (and not primarily so) but intellectually, theoretically, personally, and therefore, of course, politically, since, after all, what is politics really but the way we live with other people? ... Indeed, Stickney doesn't sound like many American poets of her generation, of any gender—these poems layer satire upon their sincerity. They substitute punch line for epiphany; they wrap knowledge in a joke; they sigh with anticlimax at the exact moment knowledge descends. —KATIE PETERSON

I love to read the poetry of Sarah Stickney, I'm rejoicing in this first full-length collection. It's like reading the classics without the idiocy of myth, which is also true of some of the classics. *A Lion* is a book we have been waiting for if we love the ability of poetry to embrace life and introspection in one swoop of lyric space, personal space the model here, intimacy with one's own self and heart and mind and body the necessary condition for poetry and readers and relationships. This is a book full of love and travel, and some high-quality drinking, and what life is like if you are full of honesty and love and courage and are unafraid of change, unafraid to find out what you really feel and know. Then again, this is also a great book if you are interested in how places and people look and feel, places maybe you never have been, like Stickney's Italy that is sort of like Patrizia Cavalli's Italy, and then again, it's a photographer's Italy, and a fiction writer's Italy. Or you want to see a place you hurried by, unheeding of the blast of place-spirit, like the side of a downtown ritzy hotel in Baltimore. American poetry, we have been bereft of the earthy poetry-spirits of Charles Simic and Linda Gregg, and we never have had enough Ritsos, and we only have Patrizia Cavalli because of people like Sarah who can read Italian poetry, but now, thank God, we have *A Lion* by Sarah Stickney, and I'm already looking forward to her next book. —DAVID BLAIR

A LION

Sarah Stickney

MADHAT PRESS
CHESHIRE, MASSACHUSETTS

MadHat Press
MadHat Incorporated
PO Box 422, Cheshire, MA 01225

The Library of Congress has assigned
this edition a Control Number of
2024931353

ISBN 978-1-952335-75-4 (paperback)

Words by Sarah Stickney
Author photo by Ryn Delgado
Cover image by Jillian Conrad www.jillianconrad.com
Cover design by Sarah Stickney & Marc Vincenz

www.MadHat-Press.com

First Printing
Printed in the United States of America

To Aphrodite

ᾶς θελετ᾽ ὔμμες
—Sappho

Table of Contents

Introduction

It's time to talk about women again. I don't mean it's time to *talk about gender*—it's always time to talk about that. And I don't mean it's time to ask *who's a woman and who's not*—what a waste of time *that* would be, what a *joke*. That's just the question the patriarchy tricks you into asking for its own ludicrous purposes. Being a woman isn't a club, it's a fate. We've all got those, they're common as birthdays.

When I say, "it's time to talk about women again," I mean that it's time to speak about matters of this kind, in this way:

> It's hard for most women
> to be as mean as they are
> when they have been trained
> nice nice nice nice nice nice nice

("Escape")

These lines are deliciously gossipy—a kind of feminine midrash to accompany the circulating folktale of our ordinary assumptions. Their resistance feels palpable but sneaky. It's less like Jesus turning over the moneychangers' tables in the temple than a magician pulling a rabbit out from a hat. "Nice" repeats seven times like a spell until it sounds like "knife."

Poetry likes to be serious about casual matters like flowers and coffee, revealing them to mean more than they first appear, squeezing out the unconscious via the indirection of description. But Sarah Stickney's poetry performs poetry's other gambit—to be (apparently) casual about serious matters, reminding us of all the things we can't seem to be able to say even if they're as obvious as flowers and coffee. Poems of our time often (not always) offer statements of deep feeling, frequently (not always) about public issues of shared concern, reliably (thankfully not always) on a grand scale. Instead, Stickney's concise lyrics offer quick takes and sharp judgments as they make available interior conversations whose uncanny logic kicks back against civilization itself. What might be most anachronistic—and most vital—about this book is that Stickney writes as a woman interested in women, not only erotically (and not primarily so) but intellectually, theoretically, personally, and therefore, of course, politically, since, after all, what is politics really but the way we live with other people?

Stickney favors home-grown materials, but her imagination tacks towards the theatrical, producing an aesthetic, and a set of concerns, that borders on burlesque. Her poems enact little scenes, like out-takes from Molière or Friends. She laces her investigations with wit and an old-fashioned sense of the folktale and more than a dash of the absurd:

> The elaborate porcelain shapes
> at the bottom of the toilet
> are to make cleaning difficult
> she told me, because men hate women

("How the Toilet got its shape")

This poem gives a gut feeling (sorry) aesthetic shape. It dramatizes misogyny using a sense of humor as bristly as a toilet brush.

A Lion, Stickney's debut collection, says, be interested in women. Be interested in what they do. This includes what they do with (and to) men. In Stickney's poems, women metamorphose—they exercise their right to change. The lines of the revisionist gem "Reader, I Married Him" don't tumble into nonsense as much as they reveal with increasing frankness the unconscious of both gender and erotic love: "Redder, I mangled him / with my nails. Ravished, / I mapplethorped him. / Revelator, I mazed him." The photographer Mapplethorpe's walk-on role is a surprise, but no accident; it takes us into the unimaginable, the realm of female fantasy—what happens when a woman mapplethorpes a man?

While I'm talking about desire—I still think the most transgressive thing a woman can be is a lover—someone who makes the first move. You're risking humiliation. You're risking failure, which America Ferrera in the 2023 movie *Barbie* reminded its viewers was the one thing a woman could not do—fail. Admirably, when Stickney investigates eros, culture isn't her guide (why would you ask your captor how to get out of prison?), but Plato's Socrates, who insisted that being a lover brought more benefit than being the beloved. Stickney's poems keep making the first move. These poems exude nonchalance, but just as they begin to seem a little too tossed-off, they convert a devil-may-care attitude to desperation and then, cunning. Consider the title poem's definitional lines:

> Being in love is a kind of lion,
> a lie, a zoo, a bundle of sticks:
> a bale I may burn
> should I feel cold.

("A Lion")

As a study in female desire, *A Lion* spends as much time on female solitude as it does on the predicament of the lover in the world. Scattered throughout the book lie a supremely odd series of poems about staying home to watch a sinkhole instead of going out on dates. Alone, the feminine solitude experiences a full range of imaginations, from the dreamy to the grotesque: "When I'm rotting hungover, / I ask myself which limbs / I would hack off / If I cared to." In the poem "They Say Desire Requires Distance," Stickney claps back at the title's conventional wisdom with a declaration of her literary lineage and her erotic temperament: "But Ingeborg Bachman and Clarice Lispector both / set themselves on fire reading in bed."

Indeed, Stickney doesn't sound like many American poets of her generation, of any gender—these poems layer satire upon their sincerity. They substitute punch line for epiphany; they wrap knowledge in a joke; they sigh with anticlimax at the exact moment knowledge descends. They play with comic timing—in one poem, a lover's mother walks in, interrupting not sex between the two but Stickney's solitary thinking, which she regards as equal pleasure. These poems also *love* intellectual activity, they *love* thinking. I'm reminded of Linda Gregg, but also of Stuart Dischell, who soothes his tragic sensibility with a spoonful of sugar. One suspects that Stickney's true poetic compatriots hail from Italy, and that this book should sit on the shelf next to the acerbic, life-giving love lyrics of Patrizia Cavalli, the embodied extremity of Jolana Insana, and the intimate domestic interiors of Elisa Biagini, whose award-winning translation Stickney collaborated on in 2014.

But Stickney remains an American poet, born and raised in New Mexico, with ties to Alabama, North Carolina, and California. Her poems carry the sense of this country that our wiser poets do—that we're just bivouacking here, that our sense of belonging is temporary, and our story of community, fragile and full of illusions. Stickney's sensibility feels formed by a resistance to conventional wisdoms that accompanies an aesthetic love of conventions. A typically American contradiction. One insight of the poet is that resisting conventional wisdoms can feel good—it's just one of the many pleasures described here, among food and sex and conversation and art and music and reading. These are poems watching out for pleasure, "the freak appearance of my happiness," ("Wood Burning") which seems, to Stickney, equal parts transcendence and grotesquerie. Pleasure— now *that's* a great topic to put women at the center of.

—*Katie Peterson*

Earliest Conversation

The earliest record of conversation
between a man and a woman
was burnt in the library of Alexandria.
What remains is full of holes
like well-made lingerie or a Sappho
poem. In it the woman claims kin
with rain sounds and says pleasure
is a bucket of paint poured out.
She says the night did not do away
with dancing, and darkness
rubbed against its fragrant neck.
The fragment ends with *But.*

A Lion

Reality's magic show
doesn't charm us anymore
is what the graffiti outside
my first teaching job said
except it said
Lo spettacolo illusionistico della realtà
non ci incanta più
and it was my third teaching job. I was lying
in wait for someone then, too. A stranger
to look into. After. Someone
to look at me. To drink my wine.
When Noah's sons cover him
they are asking not to know
what my mother thinks
of my father's mistress.
The curly parsley in the backyard
survives the first couple
frosts, but whitens afterward
like the coat of a bored lion.
Being in love is a kind of lion,
a lie, a zoo, a bundle of sticks:
a bale I may burn
should I feel cold.

Begin from Zero

To start a fire, you have to take out the old wood,
empty the ashes, begin from zero
like you mean it. I abandoned my last pair
of cowboy boots with holes in the soles
by the high-water of the Mississippi
in Memphis. I left my white linen shirt
in a motel trash can in Shawnee, Oklahoma
because it had also torn. I tossed the tank top
that reminds me of loving Patro
by the San Petronio hot springs
into a dumpster in Nashville. Turning
off I-40 onto 285, each cloud was alive
with its own unique proposal for how
to live the sky. Railroad ties held
their cheeks to the cheeks of the earth
and the patient train cars sat on them,
waiting like last night's drunks, now
sober, for the morning jailer to let them out.

Stockings

A girl in the park bites this big,
yellow tomato, and it drips all over
her sundress. I think how each woman
has a clitoris like cochineal
at the bottom of a cedar chest.
When I'm rotting hungover,
I ask myself which limbs
I would hack off
if I had to. Under my clothes
hides the animal, soft
as milkweed seed that floats off
to grow another solitary plant.
A pair of my stockings smells
of aftershave, but no man has come
to visit me. Perhaps a stranger
broke in while I was out
and standing naked in the middle
of my bed, placed those sheer
leg-shapes over his head.

Escape

You counted wrong
said my mother to my father
as we divided up Christmas cookies
we baked for friends and there weren't any
left for us. She is always glad
when we have to give away
something we really want.
It's hard for most women
to be as mean as they are
when they have been trained
nice nice nice nice nice nice nice.
What a vengeful pleasure it is
for the bartender when she flips the lights on
at the end of the night, returning us
to whatever we came to escape.

How To Let Athens Burn

Be ready to leave. Teach
the self to ford the stream
and not look down. Down
fell Eurydice. Down fell
Persephone. Down fell Dido
in flames. I say *flâneuse*
you say *lazy*. You say *placate*,
I say *crazy*. It will take
a refiner's fire. At times,
too unsteady even
for coffee, you must place
the self in a sheath. Release
when desperate. Be ready
to breathe the night
completely, you
prisoner. Be as dead
as the star, as shining.
Your future. The vault
above as blue as any
flame. Is it guilt or release
you feel just before sleep?
A lever. A meeting
with morning like
an empty beach.

Turtle

I have to try
not to fall in love
with the turtle in the aquarium:
it's the only other creature
in the room.

The Sinkhole

I invited a stranger to fuck me. I thought
let me see out this window. In the 7/11
we shook hands. He looked nothing
like his photo. I was a carnival
of myself. My first thought was *goodbye,*
but I invited him up my four flights
of stairs. I looked at the wilting daffodils
I would have thrown out
had I thought him an aesthete.
Why am I telling you this?
I was less moved than when I watch the sinkhole
from the window. When it first opened
it tried to swallow the whole street.
Now they keep it in a strait-jacket
of scaffolding. Feed it medicine
with cranes and dump trucks.
The street is still impassable
and they haven't filled it yet.

Cakes

In Baltimore I bought no dresses.
I sat in the dingy bun shop
where I watched my tinder
matches order coffee IRL.
I hadn't showered or made moves
to impersonate the self I thought
I wanted to be, so I cowered
over my tea. There is no high place
to climb in that city. Instead,
the red neon sign for Domino Sugar
can be seen from anywhere across
the dirty, pretty water of the harbor.
All I had was hunger
for the sugar of love
or attention
or just plain unmetaphorical
sugar as it pours out of combines
and into the sacks that sit
snug and heavy, waiting
to be transformed into
cakes and cakes and cakes!

They Say Desire Requires Distance

But Ingeborg Bachman and Clarice Lispector both
set themselves on fire reading in bed.
They slivered and disbranched,
red leaves released
to polyphonic fall.
My training is in longing,
so I visited the library
where a lock of Plath's hair
wrapped in plastic is preserved
in the archive. I expected
a charming blonde curl,
but it was a hank of hair
as long as my forearm.
Darker than blonde, held
in one piece with medical tape.
Even long after death, even
in a library, the body is frightening,
ungoverned.

Freudian Aliens

The alien anthropologists who study us
have discovered the airline magazine.
They file the medical ads under "zombie,"
understanding the highest erotic fantasy
for any current earth-dweller
is to have its brains eaten out.
I too like a little violence
in my love-making. A nice choke.
This is what owning a cat
is about: having something you love
to touch. I came, last night,
purely from petting, as I often do
but that's my secret. Just
as other women hide their lack
by faking, I hide how much pleasure
the man brings me. I do not give it to him
in sounds from my mouth.
I keep the electricity
in my body. I arrange myself
like an octopus over the face
of my delight. I dismember it
and suck it up.

Sinkhole: Parking Ticket

I woke up and thought something
is going to happen today, and that thing
turned out to be a parking ticket!
I considered the path of the psychic:
neon hand in the window. I grew up
under a witch, though she used
her powers mostly for the supernatural
work of raising two children, not
for cash. So I gave up
that future. I love canceling plans.
A man was going to pay me
to beat him, but I stayed home
to watch the sinkhole. After a while
I soaked my cut finger, cried,
and went to bed. Where,
in this poem, is the part
where someone whispers of figs
growing heavy and dark
in the garden, I wondered.
But by then it was quite late, quite far.

Rye Flip

Late afternoon rain took me
to a dim stool. The bartender
cracked an egg on the dark wood
between us, and let it fall
like a kissed mouth into her cool
metal shaker. She left me
and my golden drink
alone. I think of sex as many
times a day as they say a so-called
man does. If the sun isn't watching,
the moon is the pocked ground
of my desires. When I bang
through the dark to the bathroom
at night I draw back my lips
to show it my finite, animal teeth.

Zelda

Orange leaves ferment
on the sassafras trees
in front of the sanatorium—
now a fancy hotel—
where Zelda Fitzgerald
burned up. *Stupid woman,*
I thought to protect myself.
Down the street a living woman
blows kisses to passing vehicles.
I never used to see these frail,
strong people. Now at Ingles
I watch them wheel the smaller
cart carefully leaning for instant coffee
or cans of corn. They don't expect
anyone to reach the high shelf.
And I! Who pride myself
on noticing things was unaware.
But I now have what they have—
I can see it in the extra moles
and freckles that mark my skin,
like pebbles a flood has swept into the road.

Guest

Staying with friends I felt embarrassed
by my love for them, as if it were a wound
that might bleed onto their pale, hand-knotted
carpets. Home again, I filled the kitchen
with early daffodils. Lured into blooming
by the sky's fetish blue, then nearly
ruined by late snow. I need
the sound of fire
as much as I need its warmth.
Fire, my good dog, my work-shirt.
Everything living holds heat,
even the long, cool leaves
of plants. Wind blew in a poem,
and then outside all day
as if it were starving flame.
Who knows how the wind feels
about its job of touching everything.

Summer in San Vitale

The city empties roasting pavements
to be alone with its church bells.
Heat fills every crevice, and the distant
sky flows above each avenue. I must find
my stolen bike. Old men emerge
out of the back rooms of their shops
and shake their heads. At last my machine
appears on the internet for 70€. I say
I'll give you 25. When we meet outside
city walls, the two teenage crooks
are so young they're eating candy.
They take the money, and leave
with their hands in each other's
back pockets. By now the moon
is rising over cornfields where partisans
ate stale bread soup during the war.

Poem

Sappho taught me the best part
is the misery that follows
those nights in which you burn.
Of course, most nights
you won't remember
just as you don't remember
the daily tying of your laces,
or those times you briefly
take your heart out, because
it might rain. Because now
it is raining.

Any Other Lord

> *Poetry is always saying good-bye. It says, your dreams are leaving town,*
> *and not even Byron can prevent it, nor any other Lord.*
> —Kenneth Koch

I want to be all open like a singing
throat, or the face of a bee
as it tells a fellow bee
the location of a blooming
chestnut. I imagine God
sometimes as a tycoon
renting me pleasure.
Whose hot lips
have pressed which limbs
I wonder
at dinner parties.
At twilight
you do what you can
which is almost
*nothing.** About skin
imagination
is the best policy,
maybe: a gradual, velvet advance.
Sugar spilled
on the kitchen floor.

---

* A quotation from the first lines of Jon Anderson's poem "Memory: A
Vision"

The Wishing Well

From places that belong to spiders
and their crops of dust
come doubt, and the regrets
that brush against us when we sleep.
I put my hand casually
on the electric fence
thinking it wasn't live.
But it's all live. Cows
are supposed to be dumb, but
when we gaze at each other
their eyes are planets from other
solar systems; they know things.
They wait for me like a parent
waits for a child's first word. But
the moment they look away they forget.
They move together as if by appointment
to another part of the field where
they lie down and rest the weight
of their skulls on the earth like boulders.

All-Nighter with My Sister in It

We are more and more alone
as we grow older, said Amelia
in answer to a question I have forgotten
as I have forgotten all conversations except
for those few like orange peel
tossed out a car window to shrink
by the roadside. There are no good metaphors
for moving forward, especially not the road
though I like driving across this country
thinking of how many things I would change
in my life. My life! My sister Amelia
has grown kinder with time, but
more private. She drives to Denver
to get her hair dyed its original
blonde. Envious of her bright curls
all my life, even I don't want to see
them darken. I never thought we'd be older.
I was going to stay in one place
and she'd grow, like wisteria, to meet me.

How the Toilet Got Its Shape

I dread the days before Thanksgiving
in which we bleach and scour and iron and starch
and set the chairs out in the sun. Boil
another pot of water and rip new rags.
It is a burning out. An exorcism. *No one*
will notice this, I used to say to my mother,
wiping the chair legs with lemon oil.
I'm a wreck! she declares with glee,
exhausted from scrubbing the grout
between tiles with Bon-Ami on a toothbrush.
She imagines herself in the center
of a circle, and draws a red X right through.
She's told us her secrets, but Amelia and I
can't get the sheets as clean. She's often
sleepless. The elaborate porcelain shapes
at the bottom of the toilet
are to make its cleaning difficult,
she told me, because men hate women.

Sinkhole: Nightsweat

I wake and place two fingers
on my sternum, feel the sweat
that pools. Low melting point
means a material less pure,
but you knew that about me
already. I sleep again, rocked
by passing trucks that shake
the walls. Perched on the edge
of the sinkhole, I wish the apartment
would fall completely in. I see
one little steeple through my window,
one little window through my chest.
They placed a pane of glass
in a cow's stomach to see
how digestion worked
which horrified me as a child
though the babysitter who told me
thought I'd be delighted.

Halfway House

Spring checked himself back in
to the halfway house, feeling
guilty over the blooming trees
he coaxed open then froze
with late snow as he crash-landed
his warm weather jag. Spring
speaks regularly at group meetings.
He explains family members
on both sides struggle with mania.
Women have always liked me,
Spring says with his soft,
full mouth, and the women
around him in folding chairs
feel the sweetness of opening
the fridge just before a binge.

Wood Burning

During my shout-colored, ramshackle
twenties, I prayed to the 5 cypresses
at the ⅔ mark of my 3-mile walk home.
I wanted to belong to Aphrodite
like they did. My wood-burning stove
should have come with a warning; not
for the full-time job it was to stay warm
in winter. But for spring when I quit
gathering kindling, stopped sleeping with hat
and socks and two sweaters, started
taking showers because it wasn't too cold
to stand naked. In the ecstasy
of warmth, I unfurled like new leaves,
like buds released. All night in the meadow
I stayed up with anyone who cared
to drink wine, and all day sipped
tiny cups of coffee until I shook.

Mailbox

Saturday evening filled up the bar
as over the plains of the black earth
desire came, undoing her hair
pin by pin. I was drinking alone
and wrote a letter that said *I am
in love with you.* Dropped it
in a mailbox on my way to a friend's home.
Dreamed in the pelagic subway light
of the strangers passing on the other track.
Now Sunday, my words wait in the dark.
Tomorrow they will make their way
toward you like the worm we found,
transplanting herbs. I'll love you like the unicyclist
loves his single wheel. Like a three-year-old
her party shoes: Darkly, and for my own
purposes. You're the standing water
I need to cure my wart at midnight.
You're the miles of underground copper wire
through which to transmit my voice.
I am a cockroach-souled schemer,
abandoning you in the privacy
of my body as it sits in the bath.
This is my century, cheating
and ready to choke.

Reader, I Married Him

Redder I mangled him
with my nails. Ravished,
I mapplethorped him.
Revelator, I mazed him.
Or rather I martyred him,
rendered him unto Caesar.
Ref, I maxed out the clock.
Renter, I amortized. I
realized I misunderstood him
completely. Ragdoll
that I am, I merged
with him. Ravenous, I munched
& munched as I thought of him.
Reckless, I margarita-ed
to revenge myself. Rolfer,
I mashed the flesh. Rancid,
I minced and pickled.
Rampant, I manxed him
and O Romeo, I unmanned him.
In revels, I maimed us
both. Radical, I mapped
each lie and line
until there was nothing left to mar.

On Being Hit By A Bird As A Child

He's since come to believe it was only a bumblebee. But he
renews his vows to pessimism daily. Nervous
around cars, suspicious of people. Am I the first
since his mother to soothe him? We didn't stay to hear
the jukebox play the songs we'd paid for
at the Communist's Daughter, but I'm sure the girls
in summer lace haunched around the dancefloor.
We sang ourselves back to Dragon Alley.
Failure followed us like the odor of bacon
on a line cook. I'm less fucked up than you are
said the spider to the upside down beetle.
What is uppermost, and most easily hit
is the jawbone, the temple, the flat-sided cheek.

Companionship

O dark bell, my herd
of plums on the counter.
Your thin skins dusted
with white yeast
smell like marc drunk
in the dead of winter
in a chalet small enough
anyone can hear anyone
sigh, cry out.

Diagnosis

The pH test for soil reveals
I'm wonderfully dark, but too acidic.
He's the blade and I'm the thicket
that will grow back overnight,
an otherworldly color like the listerine
he brought and forgot in the bathroom.
What are these noises? he asked. *They're pleasure*
I wished I didn't have to say. He looked good
when I dressed him in my clothes, like an Italian,
and I liked him better. I slept all night
as soundly as a devil in a fire.
That we marry to drag the other's corpse
graveward is what I think, but I
am unmarried, so whether it is like being dogged
by an unshakeable sugar-craving,
or like walking on a drift
of hand-sewn snow, I do not know.
I never see farther than the ends
of the long bandages
of hope I am unwrapping.

Oedipus

Waking from the wheelhouse of a nap after
after-lunch love with his wife, the king feels
not quite right. He rises to her blank look,
to love-bites turning bruises. Unbalanced
on his weak feet, the back of his skull
buzzes like distant bees. Her whiteness.
The cool, pale fingers that would have washed him
as a child had he not been tossed
by his pierced ankles onto a pathless hillside,
pluck at his fastenings. The possibility
of a legitimate life is as thin as the spider's thread
that drops from the rafters. Hot outside,
and has been. A dream. Stinking Thebes.
Didn't he miss, by the merest shiver,
being the happiest of men?

I Dislike The Ravens

They like the last tree at the end
of the dusty lane. It's the tree I would choose
could I fly—bleak, in its leaves,
with their cries. They named themselves
for being ravenous. Fatter
than the full moon, blacker
than bark charred by wildfire,
they have no measure, are not here
for beauty. When they open
their beaks as curved as the world,
the emptiness of the desert
increases. Their croak is a horn
cracked by nightfall. Passing their tree
I saw a fight and watched one
fall. Like other prophets
they will never die as hunger
never dies but takes all the forms
of the throat: the thunder of heat-heavy
afternoons, hollow needle,
peachless peach tree. I see no nest
nor love-making.

Sinkhole: Flaw

The sinkhole is my oldest friend
in Baltimore. O sinkhole
I washed my hair
for you. I put on make-up
to watch trash blow around you
and the dump truck pour sand
into you. Suffering
is a teacher, I know, but what is it
a teacher of? Come, my flaws,
you are welcome. Come to my bathtub
and bed. I'll not abandon you
like I've been trying so hard to do.

From a Season

His only real friends, said someone
of Cézanne, *were trees.* The spindly
pines windy and free inside him.
Leaving the gallery I wished
the married man would text.
I was bringing my mother groceries
but distracted I drove the wrong way
so parked at the little park to watch
a roller skate girl groove
over the tennis courts. I, too,
love trees. I love not beauty
but revenge. I googled "why
am I attracted to married men?"
then hardly glanced
at the glowing screen.
Beside my mother's door
bloomed the last, red
nasturtium of summer.
One morning soon first frost
will shuck the plant and leave
its pale stems skewed. *Don't think*
he finally said, *that this in any way
can lessen my desire for you.*

The Beautiful One

Together & bodiless
before birth, my sister and I
decided she would push
the heavy, wooden wheel
of beauty. I wanted
freedom, and she was kind.
OK, I said, *I'm going—*
to smell mock-orange blossom,
to see a palm tree. I'll be there
soon she said,
and we said, *don't forget,*
don't forget.

The Wide Jordan

As I turned the curve of the road
I came upon an aging woman
who looked unhinged with her balding
half-dyed-black white hair, standing
in her yard askew, but then we talked
about how the mouth of a cockroach
moves, how the budding star magnolias
got burnt with frost, and I knew
she wasn't crazy, just worn away
like water wears stones smooth.
Each time our conversation might
have ended, she picked it up again,
shook it out like a fresh top-sheet.
She kept taking little steps toward me,
but never crossed the wide Jordan of her yard.

Gentian

I do sometimes hear my name called
very clear & distinct when I'm perfectly alone.
I did not leave behind any of the beliefs
of my childhood, but buried them
like a few silver coins in the mountains
where the gentian grows.

When I Put My Nose on His Nose

I can see only one eye, gas-range
flame blue, like the sky behind
orange clouds at sunset. It's the eye
of a sea-turtle, strong from his travels
through fathoms of dark water,
the secret of him alive
like a barnacle on cold rock.
On bad days he drags
his lithe body like lead.
But relaxed he stills.
I watched the planes
of his face and fine neck,
tender where it meets
the shoulder as we sat
in the tub. To fit we slid
each leg next to the other like
sardines in a tin. We had just
come in from the cold
of the October beach at evening.
Inside it was warm, no wind.
I cupped handfuls of hot water
to pour down his knees
and listened to the fall of it:
quiet, small echo of the great restless sea

Dating Advice

Don't ask him if he wants to see you again.
Don't drive to Arlington if he doesn't drive.
Don't wear your favorite earrings.
Don't dwell on lack of compliments.
Don't get into bed without knowing whether he's married.
Don't take him to your favorite bar.
Don't ask for whom he voted.
When he lends you a book
don't imagine he wants to see you again.
Don't let him pay.
Accept the knitted, homemade mouse.
Don't analyze the compliments.
Don't show him where you live.
Don't cook.
Let him pay.
After three months of good sex don't assume he'll want to see
    you again.
If you're at trivia night try to win.
Don't count on him keeping his boner.
Don't share a yoga studio.
If you want to look back on it later, try to say a couple honest
    things.

Fingertips

I meant to
masturbate twice yesterday
but both times
I fell asleep
first, the hands
of the bed
pulling me
underwater. I am always
changing places
with my captors.

Sarah Stickney

Neon Ballad

You may drink alone
as long as you don't speak about it.
You may take any quantity of pills
as long as you show up to work.
You may have sex with the worst partners
as long as you spend a lot of money
en route to said sex. If you have breasts
we kindly request that you show them.
Or that you grow fat enough to hide them
permanently. The fluorescent light
of the superego is to remain on
at all times. You can't be free
Europe often says to America.
And we say yes, yes
we can: U-S-A, U-S-A, look—
we're doing it right this second
buying take-out coffee buying juice
buying plane tickets buying gifts
buying therapy buying weekend retreats
buying the best wine from all the hillsides
of the world, buying foreclosed houses,
buying binding clauses, buying blind
alleys really trying hard
to buy sleep.

Behind in Love

To get down to the business of love, unfortunately
I can't set a timer and knock it out
like other things that freak me. Birth defects!
Communication! New studies
on lemmings! *Set a timer for 60 minutes*
Nick said during his brief but searing
period of unemployment. I do thirty
because the dung beetle is my spirit animal.
And the snail. Bonanza! Disarray! The feral atlas
of the world! I'd like to lose
one pound a week from now until
all the right things happen. Envy! Hopelessness!
A pink feather boa on the shoulders of a boob!
The powerball is up to one billion dollars! It's strange
to enroll in the ranks of humans. Aristotle says *words*
are symbols of mental experience and I say *why not*
things and my student says *well,*
because your mind is the limit of what you can know
and therefore name. Why would I want
anything else, when here I have all this lush solitude
like a chocolate river fizzing off
into a golden doughnut sunset. Famous rappers!
The last polar bear! A future neurotic
conceived in a closet this very day! I would like
to have been born when more of the world
was unknown, when ladies kept ocelots, and other Parisians
walked their beautiful tortoises in the arcades
as a symbol of calm refinement.

The Definition of a Cocktail

says my boss, is a sour, a sweet,
and bitters. Wake up
with yourself often enough
and you will be. If the meniscus
doesn't hit the jigger edge,
the drink's no good; this
is medicine. *Pick your poison*
I don't say; I hate lines.
The only poem I have memorized
anymore is "The Albatross," and
when the black dawn comes
I clutch the pillow and say,
ce voyageur ailé,
comme il est gauche et veule!
The boss is to marry an heiress
who once came into the bar.
To meet those people you have to believe
in those people. I don't care
whom I meet as long as they save me
from my future,
or at least put it off, like when I heard
the little sound of water flowing
in the stone drinking fountains
like a light left on in the house.

---

* from Charles Baudelaire's poem "L'Albatros"

Who Else

This snow lies light as salt
and more sparkly, like the hair
of a princess if hair
were different and princesses
also. I don't think much
about aliens, but I like thinking
they must be very different
than we expect. A single flake
of snow or a needle
of pine might be their size.
The daddy long-legs
who crowd my house corners
could be intelligent, ardent
guests whose many attempts
at communication have failed.
They sacrifice themselves
to my vacuum on the rare
occasions I decide to combat them.
The rest of the time they continue
to live in the fervent hope
I might misunderstand.

Leap Day

The amaryllis on the table grows slowly. February won't have
a 29th like it did last year when I went to Patro's wrapped
in my tightest black dress, careful not to muss
my stockings on the many sharp parts of my bike
as I pedaled. I arrived midafternoon
as he was making perfect pasta
on his Bunsen burner. How I fevered for his touch
when I didn't have it, imagining him with the other
Sarah. He knelt before me to kiss my sheer stockings.
He ran a hand slowly up the back of my calf
the way you might pry loose a floorboard,
or find a tied-up dinghy and take it out
to sea. We stayed in bed as if the day
were slipped between the others, a secret,
like the film they put over your passport
if you visit Havana. No one knew where I was.
I didn't add the day to my long list of sins
and bad decisions. It stayed hidden
like a heart murmur, an invisible
and mostly painless, defect.

The Present

Sometimes I'm surprised
by the freak appearance of my happiness
like a familiar face
in a soccer stadium before waving arms
erase it. I break
into applause wondering how much butter
to put in the sauce.
In another version of enlightenment
touch is taste
and taste is godly and invisible. Oh wait,
that's this one.
Even the Pope is rumored to be good-natured,
though crooks
are the most good-natured of all, sticky
with the juice
of money. The barista deftly scoops cream
with her spoon
from the neck of a heavy milk bottle.
The moment.
We call it ships on fire, undiscovered
vestigial limbs,
Lavoisier vowing to blink three times right after
being guillotined.

The Other Sarah

When he left me for a girl with my name
I became psychic. I could tell which strangers
had been betrayed as I stared into their faces
at the post office or watched them
lift espresso to their lips. I wore my hands
on my wrists so well you'd think
they grew there.

The Moon in Pointe Shoes

woos its chorus of clouds. Delicate
monster. It has been high and white since it rose
like a mother looking for a child's
lost shoe. In the ditch-park, a missing woman
is tacked to a tree in a photocopy. Her age
in the photo eighteen, or forty. I could be
eighteen or forty as winter dumps hormonal drugs
into my veins: more interior days. Examine every detail
like it's a choking hazard. *You have the voice
of someone alone in a big house,* said Rosie.
From room to room I watch the moon
move like the pit of a peach
as the fruit rots away. I think of the next
man. Of course I want pleasure.
But when I stole away to the guest bed alone
to touch myself, it was so much sharper
and thicker than the obliging shudder
I produced for a partner. *You're so handsome,*
I told his dog.

Sinkhole: Future

Vultures sitting on the shot tower
leer over the sinkhole's plastic perimeter.
Our local abyss. Workers warm their hands
in the whoosh of flame they've set
in a steel drum as the trees
cut off the last oxygen to their leaves.
Oh, it's better than freezing to death,
doesn't hurt. The men sometimes attach
a great claw to their crane and lower it
down. The sinkhole has no end
of appetite. Sometimes they tie on
a wrecking ball and let it swing.
The sinkhole knows about the future,
but won't tell. Occasionally,
looking down at it, I want
to sleep naked for old time's
sake—and time is the oldest—
remembering how slight
is this skin that can be stroked,
or soaped and wet by water
before it thins and breaks.

Tennessee Stud

Under grumbling clouds we heaved up hills
then coasted down the backside to save gas.
Patro sang "The Tennessee Stud"
in his yellow rain slicker all through
the dark Appenines. Behind him
on the Vespa, I thought about
the moving self in the moving body
of time. Animal in an animal as William Harvey
says of the beating heart. By the time
we were pressing salty anchovies
onto soft bread in mosquito paradise,
it was late. We found hotsprings
to hush the mind until only flesh
and sulphur mist remained. We were sunburnt
and often cold. Flies flocked to our stink.
The road extended its long tongue
and we stuck to it for a month
of poppies as the nightly orchestra
of fireflies played to their lost loves
in the Milky Way.

Transit

We couldn't always be together, no not
always, usually not, in fact never.
"Further more shopping beyond"
cooed the concourse pretending
to guide me. A few days later in bed
with Bukowski in bad Italian,
I was waiting for him to come back
and find me naked, when instead
it was his mother whose key
I heard turn so sure in the lock
of the door. A mother
calls the name of her son like so—
like so hard—like nothing
a lover will ever.

Call Me

Compass aspin, I slipped
into the bartender's bed, an aspirin
to soothe the headache
his fiancée gives him. Apart
from a generous cunt,
I have two wishes:
to be loved and left as alone
as the new June grass growing
so fast it is a whole man's job
to mow it. "Woulda-coulda-shoulda"
said the city employee again and again
to the DWI class I was sentenced to
on Saturdays. A fu-manchu-
sporting classmate called me Farah Fawcett.
Or Sarah Bernhardt; I don't remember.
When you are young,
a man will call just about any name
so he can call you.

Salty or Sweet

Red appears in the leaves like some Jesus
come to preach the paradox
of bright death. I can't believe
in this life or the next that I will be
as joyful as the swallows in their
swooping dives. Life's not
what I thought it would be,
I keep whispering to friends
and they agree. We are all
up at dawn, wandering the kitchen,
bitter as pith. I miss the smell of snow
when I was young. Or the smell of snow
plus the smell of dinner, which was the smell
of home. *Would that it might have pleased God*
to give us the power to understand everything
through instinct and sensibility, says Pascal.
Next time I'm going to come back
as an insect. I'll devote myself to building
a small habitation in the last magnolia
bloom in the magnolia tree by the pool
on the last day the condo pool is open,
please God.

Persephone

She's smart enough
to know she has been spared
the disappointment of endless
summer days. Family-oriented
but barren. Optimist
without hope. The prepared story
always failing, while the windy one
that skids across a field like chaff
is difficult to speak. It cannot be sliced
in half like a chioggia beet. She's as pale
as the inside of an onion now
in that cloudy, downer world.
It's been a long time,
but her memory of the sky
is not so distant, either,
like the sparkle of a gold
earring in the bottom of a pool
she once broke into.

Sinkhole: Face

The desire to understand what my face actually looks like
is misguided. Dead-Center-Adult face. The-Fun-
is-Over face. Sex-Will-Now-Be-About-Ignoring
the-Fucked-Up-Parts-of-Each-Other's-Bodies face.
Concentrating-Really-Hard-on-Something-Basic
face. Maybe occasionally Face-of-the-Monkey
on-The-Monkey's-Face. But never again the Face-
of-Petals, the Flying-Dream-Face. I flee
head-down for the next grocery aisle
at a glimpse of my perfectly pleasant
acquaintances, or even the people
I sail around calling my friends.
I want only to quietly gather
my binge ingredients and get back home,
to turn the heat too high and watch the sinkhole.
They're working on it through the night, now,
big klieg lights, and a tent to hide its mouth:
Giant and tender. I must have slept once
with my mouth wide open like that. Some solitary
animal crawled down my throat and made its home
inside me. Now it bad-dreams my blood
into dirty water running over the floor.
I must wash it hot, hot, hot, or the lonely
stain will never come out.

The Westin, Annapolis

The backside of the luxury hotel
looks ill at ease, like a person
who gathers her things to leave a hospital
after being diagnosed without cure.
The new wife on the first night
of her honeymoon has just dreamed
of losing a limb. Her husband, nervous,
makes a joke. The soft cloth of morning
is a little torn. But they will cover each other
with sunscreen, and eat crab-cakes together
downtown. For now, while he shaves
she stands on the balcony, running
through feelings to feel
when traveling. In a high place
it is perfectly typical, banal even,
to want to throw oneself off.

A Formal Feeling

Emptiness expands between an event and whatever
follows it. Spilled coffee soaks the floor mat
of my newly quiet car. Evening begs a soundtrack
for living's mania, for buyer's remorse. No, not those—
for the famous "formal feeling." A good dramatic instinct,
like fine bones in a horse, improves the journey. At the hotel
lift-off where the room's paint job was unfinished, the clock
read the wrong hour as if it were interpreting a dream. I wanted not
room service but to have eaten nothing. I wanted two years ago,
but the hours moved forward in the usual fashion all night long.
Go back and think about those things you said and felt he said.
He swallowed his tooth at a diner so authentic the literal tabletops
were greasy. We cried a little and kissed lots and then
twice more before the plane. Not a concord. Me to return
to the DC of what it might be like to have money
for tiny food and fancy blankets, my boots eaten by NYC salt.
To see the Washington water from its important bridges
was a grand gift of the light. A sheaf of wheat bending
to please return to being alone.

Sinkhole: Autumn

Now bright and passive, the fallen
leaves snazz up the ever-flowering
trash that blows around the sinkhole,
while the liver and kidneys persist
in removing the usual poisons.
You know what time it is,
says Paul to the Romans.
No day without lament; I mean
don't forget to wear your helmet:
the inside separated from the out
by just so much. Eat again.
Or have sex. I tried on
a white dress I last wore in Italy
and it didn't wrap my ribcage.
It's hard to know how to avoid lies.
To be gracious. To light the candles.
Not to think of what you could do
to your body with a toolkit.

Dip Him in the River Who Loves Water

Tell me what beast is most erotic
for I'm sure I had its form last
lifetime unless I was a nun
and all that's left of boundless love
for God are these glowing coals
between my legs, this bovine solemnity
I wear like an ugly sweater. My over-
serious heart. My first love
was not a whale. Bigger
and wetter than any whale, he married
this past weekend. I learned orcas
are actually dolphins. What a disaster!
*Love should be useless
and delightful,* said the man
I didn't bring as my plus one.
But the wedding—the wedding!
I was going to tell you everything.
I was going to give you the napkin
on which I scribbled something nasty
about someone perfectly decent.

You Often See the Shadow of a Raven

before you see the raven.
This one can neither eat
nor rest, nor put the flesh
down from its beak.
In Genesis fish and birds receive a special blessing
because there are no paths through air
or water. Every journey must be new.

Evening, Fall

The clouds talk dirty to the sycamores
until the fervent leaves shudder
down. Early dark closes over
town like a mouth
as dark as the muscle
where your blood mingles
before it splits. This willow
seen from the classroom window
will have to sub for aspirin.
It's the season colleagues reveal
themselves by where they place
their finger-revolvers. Classic
index-to-temple type? Or wildcard
who aims into the mouth?
In a simile on love, Virgil likens Dido
to a doe, running from the arrow
lodged firmly in her side.
This makes no sense,
my student's paper says:
Dido is a queen, not a deer.
What she means is the clean,
red, sear of the new gash
is lovelier far than the constrictive ache
of healing.

Appel du Vide

Lost: Reading Glasses in this Area
says a sign tacked to a bus stop
and I imagine the blinded Oedipus
coming out of the palace, his face
black with blood. Afterward
his daughters will lead him
everywhere. For love, with love
one can survive even Thebes. I accept love,
but not because it makes me feel good:
it breaks and rearranges the fibers
like carding wool. Makes tender
the way Octopus is prepared for the pot:
by running it over multiple times
in the driveway. To purify snails
before poaching them in butter
you must starve them for one month.
There is a name for the desire
to throw oneself down from a high place,
just as there is a name
for the rapture of the deep.
There's the word others use
when they call you, but no name
for this work
in the bodies of the living.

Premeditated Happiness

for Diana Thow and Kevin Allardice

I'm not in favor of premeditated happiness
says Mandelstam, meaning it's seismic
to wake to someone's real live skin and find
we may touch this living thing, soft
as a mound of flour, delicate like holding
in your mouth a moment a moth.
Out the window the engine-dumpster band
plays slow-dance numbers, while in your private air
you eat the white almond of being together.
It's Sunday. After the long, lonesome work
of learning to use words, you may speak
into the other's tide-pool ear.
When one gives the other
the cool underside of the pillow, you make
a shade tree. Everything must change
in order to stay the same, *bisogna*
che tutto cambi perché tutto rimanga com'è
says Lampedusa and I really don't know
what he means, but it sounds so right.
You are waiting in line at a bakeshop
when you realize you can bring home to your person
the very thing she likes best to eat. The heavy
world turns elephant ballet, and you stand
in the pantheon looking up—
You order it. You carry the paper bag home.

Green

The sky closes and opens its fists as if
a nurse will draw blood, then lets go
one dark hand over the hill. Rain rolls
in the grass like a lolloping calf,
and the green air drips thawed earth,
early sprouting. The green in my mind
is a flood in the night, in my chest.
Now I have a need to kiss
the cheeks of shy patrons
who walk into the bar. By the barn
Suzy the donkey eats grass,
and in her dark farmhouse your mother
makes gnocchi. Like a picture in a locket
some pretty girl wore on what would have been called
her bosom, the stars still hang
cold as car-metal above the spring house.
But the rain is alive on your tin-roofed shack
and my heart is as full as an attic.

Sarah Stickney

Mal Pais

The snail is drawing a mountain on the beach
with its wet tail. The clouds
have shaped wave-shapes in the air
so the ocean will know how important
it is. The ocean will take the snail's drawing
like it took Maria's first wedding ring and a boot
my sister loved. Everyone I have met
in Costa Rica is Canadian and they are all
beautiful. Are any Canadian beauties
left at home? There are couples who are like
I gave her an IV at midnight every night
for three months; it was the only time
she wouldn't throw up. Today we got
engaged. Then there are couples
who are like *she makes a Costa-Rican breakfast*
for me sometimes with—what do you put in it?—
oh yeah, plantains—and it's amazing.
Once a boyfriend told me I would be like eggplant
to eat. Did he know it's in the nightshade
family? Of course he did: everybody knows that.

Yellow

When other people
say the word *loneliness,* I think *no*
that's my word.

Sarah Stickney

Pomegranate

At the medieval anatomy museum
a clitoris like a pomegranate seed
waits in the 14th-century wax woman
who used to show medical students
where a baby grows. Waits for what
precise pleasure I don't know—
Apollinaire prefers the nose,
but a seed bursts darker red
inside the mouth. The beloved's
mistake is thinking. I want to be alive—
aliver than that. The bones of lions
struck together make a fire
which is why I watch your face
so closely. Nothing is to be despised
not even the entrails of animals. Give me
a turning word, for I envy fish
their movement, and birds their bones
of air. To be shaken like a drop
where I cling by a bluer fire
than the bluest sky, I undress
and stand by the bed.

Orange

Now I'm back in the body I left
like a scarecrow to guard the crop
of my pleasure. Now the rain can come,
and the marionette bats after.
Summer melon dense and orange
as fragrant as the Sunday sheets
your mother washes for your bed.
When you cover my mouth
for the upstairs housemate, it is as quiet
as a Vermeer. A ship dissolving
into darkness at nightfall.

Sinkhole: Orchestra

Woo me, jackhammer,
you're the first violin. I do not love
the gods of my neighborhood:
black plastic bags from the bullet-proof
liquor store windows swept into the sky.
But the moon comes to the window
the same way everywhere, and I love
the sinkhole and my pretend
friends, the men who work on it.
In my sleep I mistake their rumble
for the sound of our planet in orbit.

Goodbye July

How many different ways a river moves:
it has carved out the rock by pressing
into its side. It has sorted the debris
into piles. It has sat quiet in the shallows
where the fish are so little they look
like something else's shadow. Goodbye,
July. Now that you're fraying at pockets
and cuffs, I'm starting to feel at home
in you. The sturgeon moon is moving
towards full, and even the landfill
is closed. I'd like the entrance
exam for heaven to be about trees—
which ones you knew and loved.
Could you describe them? We don't know
what wide places we have inside us
until by grieving we grow into them.
Goodbye Maya, goodbye first month
without Frances. We don't get to dictate
how other people grieve, not even
the other person who is myself,
that false witness, that teenager
liable to start fires, oh, anywhere.
The old bridge, for instance,
comfortingly defunct, weeds
blooming in the concrete.
That's July turning August, older,
the edges of the ginkgo hinting color.

Sarah Stickney

The Road

Every time I slip my card
into the gas machine's slot,
I am grateful to have money
for more miles. The only way
to stay American is to stay
on the highway. I am staying.
On the road I told the story
of my failed marriage proposal
to different hosts, three nights
in a row. Like working out
a hairball, or passing a kidney stone,
if I keep telling the story it will one day
be over. No, it is over; that's why
I tell it. Telephone poles,
skittering birds, kudzu,
truck stops with their good tools,
their useful bathrooms,
their smell of bleach and gas
and hot food hot too long.

Avery County

The evening before leaving
I shot Eric's 12-gauge
out the back of his shack
into the flourishing green
of the big June woods.
My first time with a gun—
there is no promise but lots
of intimacy, as Ashbery says
of the sea. A buzzard slopes over
the highway. Who knew
this rural fix for east-coast neurosis
was waiting for me with its dogwoods,
its poor possum roadkill,
and the high, evening clouds
that bring shy wild turkeys
up the hillside. Hegel says
the wounds of the spirit heal,
and leave no scars. But time
is just like the rest of us
and wants more drinks
when it starts having drinks at the bar.

Late Blue

By now lines of crows have arrived
in your country where the sea has such a thing
for being blue. The wind strokes the long clouds
down to the horizon. When we broke
the bed we laid the mattress on the floor
and called it *the pool*. We dozed at the bottom,
dazzled and refracted like a Hockney collage.
There was a blue to the cool smell of morning
watching the light in the shallows. At night
mosquitoes descended for ardent,
blue kisses. Only the moon was yellow,
a grain of rice in the broth of a golden risotto.

Acknowledgements

Bateau: "Transit"

Carolina Quarterly: "Avery County," "The Definition of a Cocktail," "Earliest Conversation," "Freudian Aliens," "Persephone," "The Present," "Rye Flip," "The Wishing Well," "Wood Burning"

Crazyhorse: The Westin, Annapolis

Forklift, Ohio: "A Lion"

Guesthouse: "Diagnosis," "Stockings"

Massachusetts Review: "Mailbox"

Mudlark: "A Formal Feeling," "Pomegranate"

Painted Bride Quarterly: "Guest"

The Shore Poetry: "Sinkhole: Future"

Yes: "How to Let Athens Burn"

Thank you to the many great friends, readers, writers, and loved ones alive and dead who helped and supported me in the making of this book and without whom it could never have come to be. I am particularly indebted to Robert Abbott, Maria Chelko, Will Dyar, Katie Peterson, David Rivard, David Blair, Pui Harvey, John Okrent, Caroline Picard, Diana Thow, Taije Silverman, Jaye Deshpande, David Neidorf, Ranier Amiel, FBCMM, The Crew of the Aweh, Emanuele Patronicini, Rick Ziegler, my sister Amelia and my mother and father, Susan and Cary. Enduring and enthusiastic thanks to Marc Vincenz for publishing this work.

About the Author

Sarah Stickney grew up in Santa Fe, NM, where she now lives. She has taught at St. John's College (Santa Fe, NM, & Annapolis, MD) since 2013. She taught at Deep Springs College, CA, where she helped to make the school co-educational after one hundred years of all-male education, and served as Dean for two years. Her co-translations of Elisa Biagini's selected poems, *The Guest in the Wood*, won the Best Translated Book Award for poetry in 2014, and a more complete collection of Biagini's translated work *To the Teeth* was published in September 2021. She received a Fulbright grant for the translation of Albanian/Italian poet Gëzim Hajdari's work in 2010 and has worked with him for over a decade, translating selections from all his major works. She has published translations of the poetry of Vivian Lamarque in literary journals and magazines including *Transom, Two Lines,* and elsewhere. Her chapbook *Portico* was selected by Thomas Lux as 2016 winner of Emrys Press's annual competition. This is her first full-length book.

www.ingramcontent.com/pod-product-compliance
Lightning Source LLC
Chambersburg PA
CBHW021413090426
42742CB00009B/1128